Angels Must Earn Their Wings by Helping Little Angels Like Me

CHILDREN'S IDEAS OF GOD, HEAVEN AND THE ANGELS

David Heller
and Elizabeth Heller

Kensington Books

KENSINGTON BOOKS are published by

Kensington Publishing Corp.
850 Third Avenue
New York, NY 10022

Kensington and the K logo Reg. U.S. Pat. & TM Off.

ISBN 0-8217-5156-5

First Printing: November, 1995

Printed in the United States of America

To Barry, Ilene, Carey & Aliya Heller—
With love and appreciation
for their support

Contents

Introduction

*The gates of Heaven are so easily found when we are little,
and they are always standing open to let children wander
in.*
                                                    —J.M. BARRIE

This is a book about how children picture God, Heaven,
angels and all of the spiritual possibilities they can imagine. Through our extensive interviews with youngsters
between the ages of five and eleven, we have invited our
littlest spiritual seekers to wander into the sublime subjects
of God and Heaven and present their heartfelt views on
these subjects. Through the child's religious beliefs, and
with the aid of his or her imagination, angels, deceased famous figures and great-grandparents all come alive with
surprising animation and great enthusiasm for communi-
cating with our world. A separation of Earth and Heaven
has never seemed more tenuous or insignificant!

We have discovered that children are especially fond of
angels; it would not surprise us a bit if the feeling was mu-
tual. What comes through the children's ideas loud and
clear is a fascination with the accoutrements of angel-

hood—namely those ever-present halos and wings. Children are equally attracted to the goodness and kindness that angels symbolize. But they also seem to concur with the philosophical G. K. Chesterton, who offered that "angels can fly because they take themselves lightly." Adhering to that maxim, the youngsters offer a good deal of gentle humor concerning our notion of angels and of the hereafter in general. Leave it to seven- and eight-year-olds to blend gaity and solemnity in such a delightful way, all the while maintaining a reverent attitude toward the Maker of Heaven and the sanctity of our religious beliefs. It has been an exercise in joyfulness to engage the youngsters concerning this inspirational topic; it is now our considerable pleasure to share their collection of heavenly thoughts with you.

David Heller, Ph.D. and Elizabeth Heller, M.S.

What Is Heaven?

"It's a place where you could eat all the pizza you want and never get a tummy ache."

(Marie, age 5)

"It's where girls get turned into angels . . . and then God tries to do the best He can with the boys."

(Brandy, age 7)

"Heaven is the next stop after you die—unless some joker gives you the wrong directions."

(Harmon, age 11)

"Kinda like God's home state . . . But I think He has to travel around on business too."

(Emmanuel, age 7)

"A resting place where the dead people get a second wind and then they sing Christmas carols all through the year."

(Roger, age 10)

"It's a real quiet, peaceful place where there's no bugs. . . . The bugs have their own Heaven not too far away where God spreads out a gigantic picnic for them."

(Jacques, age 7)

"Heaven is a good home for people and pets and probably even for dolls, once their owners grow up."

(Odette, age 6)

"A place where your dreams come true, if they are the kind of dreams that help other people."

(Marian, age 9)

"It's like a fancy hotel where you can stay with God and have angels as friends, and it doesn't cost you anything, except what you give from your heart."

(Bonnie, age 9)

"My mother says Heaven is anywhere two people really care about each other."

(Lisa, age 12)

"Heaven is a place for playing and praying, so what could be better than that?"

(Cassandra, age 10)

"It is a special village on a cloud that is filled up with goodness and other things you can't buy in the store."

(Dana, age 8)

Where Can We Find Heaven?

"In the sky . . . If you want to find the other place, you're going to have to do a lot of digging."

(Hallie, age 8)

"They might sell maps of it in some religious stores."

(Mary Beth, age 6)

"It's not on television, it's more in the real world."

(Zachary, age 8)

"Right next to Mars . . . I bet if we met some Martians they would be really friendly people, because they're even closer to God."

(Josh, age 10)

"I think the ministers know where it is, but God makes them swear not to tell so people are surprised later on."

(Trisha, age 6)

"It's in the grass. . . . It's everywhere that God created something."

(Victoria, age 11)

"In the Bible . . . It has good stories that show that there's no shortcuts to Heaven. . . . Well, actually, Moses did take one across that Red Sea, but that was an emergency."

(Stephen, age 9)

"Look up in the clouds. . . . You should try to imagine who is makin' all that rain and snow. It ain't the weatherman!"

(Mort, age 10)

"Sometimes Heaven seems really far away. . . . I wish we could drive to it on the turnpike and stop off there on Sundays."

(Cedric, age 7)

"Heaven might be near the stars, but you don't need a telescope to see it. . . . All you need is a lot of faith."

(Andrew, age 10)

How Did Heaven Begin?

"A volcano exploded that had love instead of lava."

(Trent, age 11)

"I don't even think Superman could have made it. . . . It had to be somebody bigger than him."

(Rob, age 7)

"Mary started it when she wanted to have a baby. . . . Sometimes women don't get enough of the credit."

(Dana, age 8)

"At the beginning of time, God made it out of some clouds and sky and maybe some leftover mountains and rivers he didn't use to make the Earth. . . . He probably did it right after he had the rest day."

(Jack, age 8)

"It was created right after spaghetti. . . . Spaghetti is important, too, because they can put healthy vitamins in you, and even spirits probably like it."

(Norinne, age 7)

"A lot of people in the ancient years were crying because their grandma's and pa's were dying, so God said: 'All right already, you win!' . . . And so he made Heaven a beautiful place and He let the grandparents stay there forever."

(Robyn, age 7)

"God had a dream and He sat down at His desk and drew up a picture of Heaven. Then some angel who was like an architect in a past life took over from there."

(Duncan, age 9)

"God was just planting some seeds of goodness and Heaven was the spot he picked to plant them."

(Simone, age 11)

Concerning Entrance into Heaven

"You have to wait your turn. . . . You can't get ahead in line.**"**

(Jessica, age 6)

"There is a registration desk when you check in. . . . It keeps Heaven real organized.**"**

(Carey, age 10)

"When you see the big gold gate with the sign that says: 'Welcome to All,' then you'll know that you're entering the Kingdom of Heaven.**"**

(Richard, age 10)

"You have to die first, get dirt put on you, and get people to miss you—that's your best shot.**"**

(Hanna, age 6)

"I heard that you might have to be nice to your brother to get into Heaven, but maybe not.**"**

(Bethany, age 7)

"You start out at the ghost stage and then, when you 'want to live a little again,' you have to give up the ghost and take a seat in Heaven."

(Dean, age 8)

"A person goes to heaven straight from the ground. . . . Your shadow is the first to find out that you are accepted, and then you follow it up later on."

(Raji, age 8)

"A few times where you help the poor and you don't ask for credit—that could get you into Heaven."

(Zachary, age 8)

"God makes the picks—but He always gives hardworking people the benefit of the doubt."

(Roger, age 10)

Is There One Special Test To Get into Heaven?

"No, God just kisses you and says: 'Welcome aboard!' "

(Peggy, age 8)

"You got to be able to pick out the Devil from a lineup of impostors."

(Nathaniel, age 9)

"You just gotta be righteous. . . . I'm not exactly sure what that means, but it's not like being right-handed, it's more like treating people the right way."

(Claudia, age 8)

"There is a test. God puts a couple of multiple-choice questions to the person about what they plan to do in Heaven, and meanwhile He checks their Earth grades in His big book."

(Carey, age 10)

"You have to agree with things Jesus said or at least most of them. . . . God leaves you room to have some of your own ideas.**"**

(Tori, age 9)

"Thank God you don't have to memorize anything to get in. . . . Getting into Heaven isn't like some schools I know.**"**

(Jackie, age 10)

"You need to do at least one good deed, make a promise to do plenty more once you get a seat up there, and you have to say it without your fingers crossed.**"**

(Byron, age 10)

"God reviews your life with you on a video. . . . Once you look up from hidin' your eyes, God helps you learn from your mistakes.**"**

(Joyce, age 11)

"You might have to answer some Bible questions, but they're easy ones, like 'Who created Adam and who got mad and turned some lady into salt?' **"**

(Bridget, age 11)

"No test. You just go to a camp director guy in Heaven and he shows you where to bunk.**"**

(Elliot, age 8)

"The only test is whether you really want to be there in the first place.**"**

(Sharie, age 11)

"I don't think God is going to test me. He knows I'm good and I think He loves me with all His heart already."

(Benita, age 7)

What Is Heaven Like?

66There are supposed to be holy streams and waterfalls in Heaven, so sometimes I wonder if there might be holy waterslides too.99

(Burke, age 8)

66They got everything you could imagine there . . . even Oriental rugs.99

(Theresa, age 9)

66The flowers and the fruits in Heaven come alive. . . . They would all sing to you when you get there except the lemons always sound a sour note.99

(Travis, age 12)

66Don't be too surprised if you run into three smart men up there who are on a first-name relation to Jesus.99

(Len, age 8)

"There's a NO SMOKING sign when you first come through the tunnel into the light. . . . In Heaven they want to set a good example for Earth."

(Greg, age 12)

"There sure is a lot of bread and fish in Heaven. . . . You would think they would get tired of it, after all the centuries, and start eating something like watermelon instead."

(Ryan, age 10)

"There is a little house you'll have in a meadow by a creek. . . . But the best thing is you will never be lonely, because you will have as many friends as you want."

(Chandra, age 6)

"Heaven is a lot like here—except God reads you a story at night instead of your parents."

(Elizabeth, age 7)

"I see John and Luke and Mark with their fishing nets. . . . They are having better luck in Heaven because the fish are eternal and they don't mind being caught."

(Duncan, age 9)

"The first thing you notice about Heaven is there is hundreds of angels everywhere. . . . Gee, those angels really do have a lot of children!"

(Michelle, age 10)

"Heaven is something like Walt Disney World, but it doesn't have Mickey or Goofy. . . . They're in a different place."

(Hanna, age 6)

"The climate there is mild. . . . But if you want snow in Heaven, they can arrange for some to fly up to you and land on your front lawn."

(Peter, age 8)

"There are no doctors or lawyers in Heaven. . . . They don't need them because God does all the healing and because all arguments are against the law."

(Lisa, age 12)

"Some nights in Heaven God just gathers everybody around and they all eat popcorn and talk about how to make our world a better place."

(Val, age 7)

On Heavenly Happenings

"Breakfast starts with a prayer and ends with a toast to goodness over evil. . . . Plus the orange juice is out of this world because it's fresh-squeezed by angels."

(Mary, age 8)

"Heaven has tour buses for all the new people. The driver says stuff like: 'On your left, you can see the garden home that Adam and Eve retired in after they got on in their years.'"

(Jason, age 11)

"The people up there look after you. . . . They're rooting for you when you try something important, like riding a two-wheel bicycle for the first time."

(Dean, age 7)

"Heaven is so peaceful that even the dogs and cats there have halos on them."

(Betty, age 7)

"Since you're dead when you get to Heaven, you might not have to work. . . . So I would probably just play soccer all the time."

(Carey, age 10)

"Every spirit has a job there. But the best job is being an angel, because you get to wear a uniform and real fancy headgear."

(Zachary, age 8)

"God is there helping kids who couldn't walk on Earth— they're standing up for the first time."

(Natalie, age 7)

"When you have soup in Heaven the noodles are in the shape of angels, hearts and halos."

(Bernadette, age 7)

"The biggest holiday is Bible Day. Everybody dresses up as their favorite Bible character, but then you actually get to meet somebody like Jesus or Jacob and you get to pray with them in person."

(Denny, age 9)

"God has a master chef. . . . But he doesn't cook for God, his job is to figure out how to feed the poor of the world."

(Mark, age 10)

"When I get to Heaven I want to be a teacher or a psychiatrist. . . . You know even angels might need somebody to listen to their worries."

(Bernice, age 11)

"Mostly just love goes on in Heaven. . . . There isn't much time for anything else, but nobody has ever complained in the whole history of Heaven.**"**

(Allan, age 10)

What Is Heaven's Number-one Rule?

"If you take a trip away, God will always leave the light on for you."

(Koby, age 10)

"Every person is considered a famous star just because they made it into Heaven."

(Trish, age 8)

"This is eternity, so take your time. . . . From now on, you're going to have plenty of it."

(Clark, age 11)

"Angels always have the right-of-way at an angel-crossing."

(Erich, age 11)

"If you aren't sure, always give the other spirit the benefit of the doubt."

(Jan, age 9)

"Turn the other cheek . . . but if you do, don't be surprised if you get kissed a lot, because that happens all the time in Heaven."

(Bryn, age 11)

"Be kind to animals. . . . One of them could be mowing the lawn next door to you because he's your neighbor."

(José, age 10)

"Last one to enter Heaven takes out the garbage . . . but don't get too bummed out, because in Heaven even the garbage smells real good."

(Rodrick, age 8)

"Nine o'clock at night is prayer time . . . so everyone gets into bed, says their prayers and then the Angel Express Delivery Service brings them milk and cookies through their windows."

(Sydney, age 8)

"The flying speed limit is 25 mph. . . . It was the only way God could keep the peace in Heaven, once some of the teenage angels started thinking they were race cars."

(Bryan, age 12)

"Respect your elders and your youngers too. . . . Every person that God creates deserves the same respect."

(Stewart, age 9)

"No changing history . . . let the people on the Earth work things out for themselves, because that's the best way for them to learn."

(Carey, age 10)

Some Things You Can Do in Heaven that You Absolutely Can't Do on Earth

"Have a picnic with a real-live saint."

(Clara, age 8)

"Kiss an angel good morning."

(Sebastian, age 10)

"You can fly to the local ice cream store and get any flavor for free. . . . On Earth, you have to walk and you have to pay for it."

(Marie, age 6)

"I think you can probably take a nap with God in Heaven."

(Camille, age 7)

"Talk to your dead relatives about how things are going."

(Carey, age 10)

"Pray—without anybody thinking you're a nerd for doing it."

(Mert, age 9)

"Float on a cloud instead of going to school."

(Allan, age 10)

"Play pin-the-tail-on-Satan."

(Jackie, age 10)

"Have a two-way conversation with your cat that isn't living no more."

(Grant, age 10)

"Eat Chinese food standing upside down. . . . I'm sure there's no gravity in Heaven."

(Marcus, age 11)

"Play beautiful music even though you are tone deaf. . . . In Heaven, if you believe you can play, then you can play."

(Yoki, age 9)

"One thing you can't do in Heaven is tattletale. . . . God won't allow that gossip stuff so I guess I better get my chance here."

(Peggy, age 8)

"You might even be able to have a family meal in Heaven, one with all your aunts and uncles, and not have one single argument."

(Joan, age 9)

"You can tell all your worries to God and have God say: 'Don't worry, my child' . . . Actually, maybe you can do that here on Earth too."

(Sammy, age 9)

The Residents of Heaven

"Gabriel plays a trumpet in the early morning and that is like your mom and dad's alarm clock. . . . It's rise 'n' shine for all the spirits."

(Marian, age 9)

"Adam and Eve are there. . . . They're angels now. . . . Finally! It took them forever!"

(Jessica, age 9)

"Priests are in Heaven, and so is anybody else who had to listen to people talk a lot and couldn't say what they really thought."

(Jack, age 8)

"My dog Harry is fetching a stick for God up there in the clouds."

(Val, age 7)

"The President who got shot in the open car is in Heaven. God told him to look after President Clinton, and try to help him make the right decisions, not just the ones that might get him votes."

(Helene, age 9)

"My grandfather is in Heaven teaching the kids there to play card games. . . . And he's makin' darn sure those kids in Heaven don't cheat either."

(Wayne, age 8)

"It's pretty much any ol' Joe who lended a helping hand to somebody else on Earth."

(Ryan, age 10)

"Angels are in Heaven doing the Lord's work—healing and giving charity. Some of the angels might be my relatives, because they could have changed a lot once they got up there."

(Denise, age 8)

"Christopher Columbus has been there for many years. . . . He found out that if you sail long enough, you can finally get where you're going."

(Evan, age 9)

"Jesus is in Heaven. . . . He leads the prayers and I think he still likes to fiddle around and do some carpenter's stuff with his dad."

(Vance, age 8)

"My grandma is making pasta in heaven and she's growing me some strawberries for when I get there. . . . I think she might have to put them in the refrigerator for a while, because I'm not even six yet. **"**

(Marie, age 5)

"Heaven is full of angels and souls and people like Martin Luther King. . . . Heaven is where the good people hang out. **"**

(Shonte, age 10)

"God is sitting in Heaven, but He isn't on a throne or anything, no sir. . . . He's sitting in a garden playing with the children and the animals and letting them climb on Him. **"**

(Cara, age 6)

A Brief List of the Most Popular Books in Heaven

"Fun Things that You Can Do Now that You're Invisible"

(Louise, age 7)

"Near-life Experiences. . . about people in Heaven who fall into holes or bump their heads and then get confused and think they are back on Earth."

(Kimberly, age 11)

"How to Lose Weight Even Though Heaven is Like a Giant Banquet with Three or Four Desserts a Night"

(Yoki, age 9)

"Traveling without a Guardian Angel: Safe Places in the Universe You Can Explore on Your Own"

(Rich, age 10)

"How to Retire Early Because You Love God So Much"

(Kevin, age 10)

"Life after Homework and Death . . . it's especially written for kids."

(Byron, age 10)

"Why the Devil Can't Help Himself: Part I"

(Joseph, age 9)

"What I Would Have Done Different in the Wilderness, by Moses"

(Beth, age 9)

"Prayers for Angels: A Top-flight List of Them"

(Sebastian, age 10)

"The Creation Thing: In Seven or Maybe Eight Easy Steps"

(Tony, age 12)

"How To Be More Patient with Your Relatives Back on Earth Even If They Make You Pull Your Hair Out"

(Ted, age 9)

"The New Heaven Exercise Book for the Newly Dead"

(Allan, age 10)

"God's Favorite Jokebook: Special Section on Priests and Their Speeches"

(Randall, age 11)

"The Study Book for Good Life Behavior . . . the only one you'll ever need, by God."

(Carey, age 10)

"Forgiving: How You Can Get Better at It and Even Forgive Your Boss . . . the one that you had when you were slaving away back on Earth.**"**

(Clark, age 11)

What Exactly Is an Angel?

"Anyone who helps me with my homework—my mom is one that I know real well."

(Bobbi, age 9)

"Somebody who plays harp songs such as *Kiss an Angel Good Morning* and other angel hits."

(Jennifer, age 11)

"A being who has two bright-colored wings and, of course, a whole wardrobe to match the wings."

(Hallie, age 8)

"Angels protect you from bullies at school . . . but I don't know how they do that since they're invisible."

(Eli, age 8)

"They have to have three things: wings, the ability to fly and yellow hair. . . . The yellow hair is so they'll stand out in a crowd."

(Jamelle, age 8)

"A person with a halo stuck on, not something phony or pasted on . . . To get a halo, you have to be a real person first.**"**

(Mark, age 10)

"An angel is a spirit that enjoys praying as much we love jumping rope and coloring. . . . Hard to believe, but it's true.**"**

(Laurie, age 7)

"Angels understand our needs even better than we know. . . . That's why they are concerned about whether we are getting enough love more than if we're getting enough candy.**"**

(Deion, age 8)

What Do Angels Look Like?

"No feet, no arms, just all heart."

(Jenny, age 9)

"They look beautiful even though they're hundreds of years old and they don't have any makeup on."

(Laurie, age 7)

"Angels are good flyers with flapping wings and probably those pilot goggles on."

(Raji, age 8)

"They could be fussy about having their halos on straight. . . . It would only be human."

(Janine, age 8)

"For some reason they always have nightgowns on. . . . Maybe they are like firemen and they have to jump up in the middle of the night and slide down a pole if there's an emergency."

(Andrew, age 10)

"I think maybe that baby angels get training wings. . . . Being an angel takes a lot of practice."

(Justin, age 6)

"Angel dresses are pink and they like to play music . . . probably the trumpet."

(Marie, age 6)

"They always look like ladies with gold and white dresses on, but the biggest thing is they have good manners. . . . They don't try to grab for food and they always say please and thank you."

(Cerita, age 10)

"Angels wear flowers in their hair. . . . It keeps them fresh even though they have to travel through nine or ten galaxies."

(Debi, age 10)

"Some angels are white, some are black, the color doesn't make any difference. . . . It's the heavenly thoughts that count."

(Michelle, age 10)

What Do Angels Do in Heaven?

66Angels have pep rallies in Heaven. . . . It gets the angels all geared up to tackle the world.99

(Greg, age 12)

66Angels are in charge of the 'Visitors' section of Heaven. They are really good at making people who just died feel right at home.99

(Malorie, age 8)

66They're God's biggest helpers. . . . But they aren't like servants because God treats them like one of the family.99

(Blaine, age 9)

66Heaven is where angels do all the planning on how to help children. . . . Teaching kids to be good is a tough job, but somebody's got to do it.99

(Jody, age 8)

"Actually, angels are like the park rangers of the whole universe and Heaven is kind of their home base of operations."

(Lisa, age 12)

"I think angels must need an address to put on their business cards. . . . Seventh Heaven is the best choice."

(Tyrus, age 9)

"When you see stars in the sky near Heaven, those are angels watching over you. . . . When you see a shooting star, that's an angel coming down to help."

(Elizabeth, age 6)

"Heaven and angels were both created by God. He needed some friends and they needed a few clouds they could call their own."

(Ryan, age 10)

"Angels sleep in Heaven, but they aren't there all the time. . . . Angels are all around us, we just have to look for them."

(Norinne, age 7)

What Instructions Do Angels Receive?

"This is God speaking. Angels, don't do anything I wouldn't do. . . . That means no overnight stops in Atlantic City!"

(Bridget, age 11)

"Make sure you store up on kindness. . . . That's the only fuel you will ever need."

(Melanie, age 11)

"Angels, don't be too hard on yourselves. Remember that a guardian angel has to watch out for burnout too."

(Byron, age 10)

"Ladies, healing is the name of our game."

(Mishelle, age 10)

"God gives the angels a road map and then they have to follow the *x*'s."

(Louise, age 7)

"Angels, I have a lot of faith in you. . . . But please be careful. . . . And remember to duck when those 747s come whizzing by."

(Erich, age 11)

"Always take the high road. . . . That's why I picked you as an angel of God in the first place."

(Joan, age 9)

"Get plenty of rest. . . . Angels need a good night's sleep just like people do."

(Daphne, age 6)

"Fly fast and go get 'em . . . and don't forget, I'm sending a little lightning to Florida today, so stay clear of there."

(Yoki, age 9)

"Obey all 613 Commandments, be nice to people, and whatever else you do, don't tell the people you are an angel . . . that will ruin the surprise."

(Carey, age 10)

"You older angels, double-check your wings. . . . If one is silver and the other is gold, we'll have to give you a vision check and see if you need glasses."

(Yvonne, age 8)

"Don't get down on yourself if you can't get people to go in the right direction. . . . Remember that they have to make their own choices."

(Jackie, age 10)

"The best advice I can give, my chosen messengers, is to let your hearts be your guide."

(Ann Marie, age 10)

Concerning the Curious Relationship Between Angels and People on Earth

"We're kinda soul mates with them."

(Jim, age 11)

"Angels are transportation for people. . . . They take us to Heaven nonstop."

(David, age 11)

"Angels are like friends that never get mad at you and always remind you to look both ways when you cross the street."

(Cara, age 6)

"Angels must get their wings by helping little angels like me."

(Laurie, age 7)

"They help people with sicknesses. . . . Angels get very sad when they lose a patient."

(Bobbi, age 9)

"They got a lot of light around them and they try as hard as they can to shine it on the world."

(Roger, age 10)

"My mother says that apples are overrated. . . . It's really an angel a day that keeps those doctors and diseases away."

(Cassie, age 8)

"Angels love us a lot. . . . It's sort of what they carry with them mostly . . . they carry love in their backpacks."

(Amelio, age 8)

"It's good to try to be like an angel. . . . Even if you're a gym teacher or an insurance man or something like that, you should give it a try."

(Alexander, age 9)

"Some of them used to be just like us. But then they died and so they got promoted and then they got raised even when they weren't expecting it. . . . It comes as a big surprise to most people."

(Sandra, age 11)

"Angels are like people in the family that watch over you when you are sleeping . . . I think they must kiss us when we aren't looking."

(Sarah, age 6)

What Would You Say to an Angel?

"How did you really get your wings? Did you have to do any dangerous miracles like catch someone who was jumping off a bridge?"

(Dexter, age 7)

"Would you like to come over and have some cake? You'll like it; it's angel food cake."

(Denise, age 8)

"Is there really only peace and quiet in Heaven, or do you angels sometimes start your own orchestra and play up a storm?"

(Robbie, age 9)

"How do you get people to Heaven? Elevators that glow in the dark?"

(Tonisha, age 9)

"I hope we have all the facts right about Jesus. Say, did he play touch football when he was a boy?"

(Lonnie, age 7)

"I heard that some angels were guardians and some were wish angels. . . . Could you introduce me to a wish angel? I need a new house."

(Drew, age 7)

"I'll trade you my headphones if you let me try on your halo. . . . Is it a deal?"

(Tyrus, age 9)

"Bring me up for a ride and let me take a look around. . . . I can ride piggyback, but just let me know when we get to the Heaven gate."

(Julianne, age 6)

"Angel, how is God? I worry about Him because people say you don't see Him around that much anymore."

(Hanna, age 6)

"Could you bring this letter to my grandma, Miss Angel? Thank you. It says 'I love you, Grandma, and I hope you are happy in Heaven.' "

(Marie, age 5)

"Do you know Psalm 23? I would like it if you would read it to me real slow. You can skip the part that's not for kids."

(Carole, age 10)

An Average Day in the Life of an Angel

"Eat, sleep and perform three or four miracles. . . . That's about it."

(Roger, age 10)

"For fun, they try to outrace doves and eagles. . . . It keeps the angels in shape and the birds like to hear about what's going on with Jesus at the same time."

(Lonnie, age 7)

"Watch people and protect them and keep score on whether they've been good or bad."

(Rudy, age 6)

"They follow around a sad person and take away their tears at the end of the day."

(Raji, age 8)

"Angels whisper baby names in ladies' ears and that gets people started on having a family."

(Bethany, age 7)

"They gather together and they gossip about goodness until dinnertime."

(Kendra, age 9)

"In the winters in Heaven, they all lay down with their wings in the snow and make 'snow angels' with the children up there."

(Trisha, age 6)

"I think those angels do a lot of dancing and kissing in their spare time. . . . They probably dance around the moon."

(Janet, age 7)

"Angels like to do paintings. . . . An angel really did that Mona Lisa painting, but the other guy took the credit."

(Duncan, age 9)

"When they're tired and they think people on Earth might be too, they make a blizzard so everybody has a snow day and gets some rest."

(Eli, age 7)

"From nine to five they do their jobs and bring dead people up to the sky. . . . At night they have more freedom, so they can take their halos off and hang their wings up and maybe have a cocktail party."

(Andrew, age 10)

What Does It Take To Be an Angel in Modern Times?

❝Laptop computers that are easy to fly with.**❞**

(Shonte, age 10)

❝Modern angels wear earrings. . . . That's the main difference.**❞**

(Bethany, age 7)

❝Just like in the ancient days, you still better listen to your mother if you want to have a chance.**❞**

(Kara, age 9)

❝You have to be better at remembering names. . . . There's more people on the Earth now, and you don't want to get mixed up and have somebody fall in love when all they really needed was to get their car started in the cold weather.**❞**

(Andrew, age 10)

❝You have to be smart about science and nature, but it's even more important to be smart about people's feelings.**❞**

(Sami, age 9)

"To be an angel now you might have to have a bigger voice because people might not be listening so good."

(Bernadette, age 7)

"Angels need to know about basketball. . . . So many people are asking angels to help their teams win that the angels have to put on their own game in Heaven first so they can decide who to help."

(Louis, age 9)

"Angels need to learn all the languages of new countries, and they have to teach everybody the language of peace."

(Cyprian, age 10)

"You have to know about kindness—it don't matter whether you are modern or old, you need to have kindness if you want to call God your friend."

(Isabella, age 8)

Angels' Favorite Sayings

"God bless you . . . even if you didn't sneeze."

(Dexter, age 7)

"Come fly with us year-round."

(Wallace, age 10)

"A halo is the best hat anybody could ever ask for."

(Zachary, age 8)

"Satan, hit the road! This is God's country!"

(Jim, age 11)

"We feel misunderstood. . . . People must think we are just here for extreme cases, but we're really around all the time."

(Lorraine, age 11)

"Another day, another kid we kept from looking at somebody else's math paper . . . an angel's work is never done."

(Will, age 9)

"Time for wing repair! . . . George, be a buddy and take over the east-coast shift for me, will ya?"

(Shonte, age 10)

"Listen to God. You can't go wrong with the man upstairs. . . . Actually, He's kind of across the hall from us."

(David, age 11)

How Do Angels Feel About Children?

"Angels think that we're cute and wonderful. . . . Baby-sitters might feel different."

(Sharon, age 8)

"They know we're close to Heaven even though we can't fly."

(Peter, age 8)

"Angels are happy when we finally grow up. They think to themselves: 'Phew . . . I was sweating that one out. I didn't know if he was going to make it.'"

(David, age 11)

"They're right there when we are born so they like to stick around for your whole life and see how it turns out."

(Cassandra, age 10)

"Angels love children the best because we believe in them the most."

(Thomas, age 8)

How Do Angels Feel About Grown-ups?

"Angels love grown-ups because grown-ups take kids to watch a baseball games and then your guardian angel gets to go too!"

(Jerrod, age 8)

"If a grown-up is the type who likes pizza and God, then an angel will get along with her just fine."

(Bethany, age 7)

"Angels think that grown-ups see things upside down. . . . They should take more of a heavenly view of things."

(Lisa, age 12)

"Angels are upset and sad when they see grown-ups having a fight. . . . The angel feels tons better when the grown-ups kiss and make up."

(Sheila, age 8)

"Every grown-up has a guardian angel . . . So that angel gets attached to the grown-up and feels like the person is like a little brother or sister to them."

(Cherie, age 8)

What Is God's Role in Heaven?

❝God is the main enchilada.❞

(Bryan, age 12)

❝He leads all the prayers and drinks all the wine.❞

(Felix, age 6)

❝Like the mayor of Heaven, but God doesn't have to worry about getting elected again. . . . He's a shoe-in.❞

(Harold, age 10)

❝He runs the Library of Knowledge and He's happy to see that the spirits are interested in getting more wisdom after they're dead.❞

(Kerry, age 9)

❝I think He makes pancakes for breakfast for everybody in Heaven. . . . And He does it every Sunday without missing one.❞

(Marie, age 6)

"God is like a parent who gives out love and leaves discipline stuff up to you. . . . By the time you get to Heaven, you should already be real grown-up."

(Jonathan, age 10)

"He watches everybody and gives them a report card every month."

(Carey, age 10)

"Sort of like a counselor to all the angels . . . He gives them tips on how to save a soul and not let the soul know what hit them."

(Marilee, age 8)

"He starts the people in Heaven in their morning exercises. . . . Like He says: 'God says, stretch out your arms'— and all the Heaven people do it like they were playing Simon Says."

(Claudia, age 8)

"He might be the one who teaches the children Hebrew and maybe Greek and Latin too . . . He likes to keep things kinda traditional."

(Louis, age 11)

"God is God and everyone else is trying to be like God. . . . He is the world's greatest role model."

(Erich, age 11)

"God runs a smooth ship in Heaven, and the people feel like they are on a cruise forever."

(Darnell, age 11)

"His main job is to make sure the word gets out to the people of the world to be good."

(Allan, age 10)

"God's role? . . . To love all the people and give them a nice home."

(Mimi, age 7)

Is God a He or She or Something Else Altogether?

"God is something like my mother except God probably doesn't cook as good."

(Camille, age 7)

"I sure hope God is a He. . . . If God isn't a He, then I'll be in big trouble for pulling girls by the hair."

(Nathaniel, age 9)

"God is a lady because only a lady could make daisies and nice roses like we have here."

(Marie, age 6)

"God is definitely a man because God loves sports and He made all the sports teams in His image."

(Ollie, age 11)

"All I know is God doesn't eat near as much as any of the he's or she's I know."

(Aliya, age 6)

"God doesn't wear a skirt or pants; God just wears a smile for everybody who wants to join God in Heaven."

(Sharie, age 11)

"God is more like the wind. . . . Did you know they have wind in Heaven? Yeah, but it's much more gentle and it never blows people around or makes them lose their hats."

(Hillary, age 10)

"They don't worry about being a girl or a boy in Heaven. . . . They just think about goodness all the time."

(Joan, age 9)

"I picture God as a big guy, but not mean like a wrestler. . . . He's nice like my social studies teacher, and He's real friendly with the lady teachers too."

(Darnell, age 11)

"I want to know if God could be a lady. . . . Then maybe I would share my cookies with Her instead of eating them all up."

(Glynnis, age 5)

"God is not a he or she. . . . God is nothing but God, and that's okay by me."

(Carey, age 10)

How Does God Communicate
With the Residents of Heaven?

"Bugle call for angels is at five o'clock sharp."

(Terence, age 9)

"God uses an overhead projector. . . . He puts information about troublemakers on it."

(Carey, age 10)

"He just talks to the people real casual. . . . He's glad they can have regular conversations without the people's hair standing straight up from seeing Him for the first time."

(Dan, age 10)

"God whispers in people's ears, and it sounds like sweet music to them."

(Tamara, age 8)

"His voice is in their radios and it says to the people: 'This is Good Afternoon with God. I'm your host, God, and today's topic is heavenly gardening. Are you having problems with your own garden? Then give me a call and I'll see if I can perform a miracle weed cure.' ''

(Wayne, age 11)

''Maybe God uses a fax machine sometimes.''

(Allan, age 10)

''Some of the communication is through prayers and some of it is through going to God's public appearances, which are always sold out.''

(Tim, age 10)

''There's no burning bush or anything. . . . In Heaven all the bushes got computerized about 1980.''

(Gretchen, age 10)

''Like, if you go to a baseball game in Heaven, God appears on a big screen and tells the people to enjoy themselves and remember not to keep score—because they should play for the fun of it.''

(Geoff, age 9)

''Sometimes God talks from a mountain. Sometimes God sends Mary or Joseph to the villages and they tell the people: 'God wants us to pray harder.' . . . And then the people have Mary and Joseph over for a fish-and-fries dinner and ask them how their son is doing.''

(Brad, age 9)

''God just calls up people on the telephone and they talk for hours . . . unless the person has Call Waiting, and so then they have to call God back later on.''

(Jamie, age 8)

A Few Very Important Things About God that Many People Overlook

"He loves hot dogs and hamburgers . . . but He won't eat them around the animals in Heaven, because He doesn't want them to get upset."

(Dave, age 8)

"He's working on a new book of the Bible, and this story is supposed to take place in Texas. . . . I guess they got desert there."

(Bernard, age 9)

"God likes to keep Heaven neat. So He asks all the people to keep after themselves, and He even goes to parks and cleans them up Himself."

(William, age 7)

"God has two left feet, so He understands when a person is not very good at something."

(Monica, age 10)

"God runs day-care in Heaven. . . . He likes to give the little angel kids his extra-special attention."

(Linda, age 8)

"God is really pretty small, but He sorta leaves a big impact on you once you meet Him in person."

(Esteban, age 9)

"He loves sinners too."

(Kyle, age 10)

"God doesn't like it when marriages get divorced. . . . He just wishes there was more He could do to help."

(Bev, age 8)

"He has a foreign-sounding accent. . . . His voice is made up of all the languages of the world."

(Bridget, age 11)

"God is a spirit and so God doesn't look like anything we've seen . . . not even like a dad."

(Aliya, age 6)

"He doesn't care if people shave their heads or wear earrings in their noses. All God cares about is whether you know how to be generous."

(Jeana, age 10)

"God is actually pretty shy . . . so I think maybe we should reach out to Him more."

(Louise, age 7)

"We should remember that God cries too."

(Simone, age 11)

What Does God Do in His Spare Time?

"Plays dominoes with a couple of his fun-loving angels."

(Tim, age 10)

"He goes jet-skiing on Lake Heaven."

(Cory, age 11)

"Sings *Rock-a-bye Baby* to Jesus."

(Bella, age 8)

"God watches Heaven Box Office on His satellite dish. . . . It mostly has movies about nuns and religious teachers."

(Alice, age 10)

"He plays with the doves and He tries to convince the hawks to be less hostile."

(Jeremy, age 11)

"In God's spare time, God still likes to help people with their troubles with pharoahs."

(Lauren, age 6)

"God takes a vacation on Paradise Island and eats guacamole and potato chips and drinks coconut juice and says things like: 'This is food for the gods.'"

(Marcus, age 11)

"I think God eats grapes a lot and maybe reads His mail and tries to figure out the best way to answer a million letters a day. . . . He may be God, but He still needs a secretary."

(Stacy, age 10)

"He does arts and crafts with the children in Heaven."

(Ruby, age 7)

"Probably God eats chicken nuggets with fries."

(Aliya, age 6)

"In His spare time, God is busy writing new prayers into people's hearts."

(Tiffany, age 8)

"If I was Him, I would lay down and take it easy more. . . . I think God must work too hard."

(Erica, age 6)

"God likes to take a walk in the forest and leave acorns so that the animals have enough to store up for winter."

(Tanya, age 7)

"God just plans for the future. . . . Right now He's probably figuring out what job to send me to, and I hope He realizes that I would like a hockey job the best."

(Jaymes, age 12)

"Even when He is relaxing God is always dreaming of a better world."

(Rebecca, age 9)

What Is the Easiest Thing for God To Do?

"Make the sun shine . . . God has that act down because He's been doin' it for years."

(Cory, age 11)

"Play Ping-Pong without ever losing a point."

(Walt, age 9)

"Think up a few extra commandments to keep the people in Heaven on their toes."

(Ollie, age 11)

"Move a mountain . . . He doesn't even need one of those big cranes, just a few hard-working angels."

(Aretha, age 8)

"Make miracles happen . . . even how to divide up the sea only took God a few minutes to look up in His notebook."

(Dianna, age 8)

"The easiest thing for God is knowing who is praying in church and who is snoozing."

(Penny, age 8)

"It's easy for Him to be perfect . . . except for munching on chocolates, which is a big weakness of His."

(Nina, age 9)

"Turning a sinning person into an angel is ol' hat to Him."

(Byron, age 10)

"I think He can change the weather pretty easy . . . but God doesn't like to make it snow in the summer because it messes up everybody's vacations."

(Karen, age 8)

"Bringing new babies into the world and making sure they are taken care of."

(Daphne, age 6)

"If the children in Heaven aren't studying Scriptures enough, it's not hard for God to push a master switch and shut off all the televisions in Heaven."

(Matty, age 8)

"He can bring Jesus back any time He wants. . . . But you know how it is—timing is everything in life."

(Patrice, age 11)

"The easiest thing is loving us—that comes natural to God."

(Tony, age 12)

What Is the Hardest Thing for God To Do?

"Find a room at the inn when He comes to visit us—the prices are still real bad, just like they were in Jesus's day."
(Richie, age 9)

"When He has to suspend an angel for falling asleep on the job or trying to sign a contract with somebody else."
(Stacy, age 10)

"Watching people have wars . . . God gets depressed when that happens."
(Meryl, age 9)

"Whistling . . . God is kinda old and He might not have any teeth to help Him make sounds."
(Leigh, age 7)

"Making the land . . . He had to do it all, and the water too, but it took Him a long time . . . at least seven whole days."
(Aliya, age 6)

"Keep His Garden of Eden in order and chase all the snakes out . . . It still is a big problem in Heaven, and they don't like to use sprays up there because of the environment."

(Brooke, age 8)

"Hardest thing? That's easy. It's giving up on a lost soul."

(Terence, age 9)

"If God is anything like my father, He probably has a hard time relaxing. . . . I recommend a warm bath every night."

(Julianne, age 8)

"It must be hard for God to wait for human beings to really understand what He is all about."

(Koby, age 10)

"He can't just automatically make people as wise and kind as He is. . . . There's no kit He can use to do it speedy."

(Stewart, age 9)

"Debate whether to send a questionable person to Heaven or Hell."

(Carey, age 10)

"Ask people to wait a little bit to come into Heaven. . . . Sometimes they don't have the beds made up and the linens changed yet."

(Jackie, age 10)

"It's hard for God to let angels do some of His work for Him. . . . God always wants to do everything Himself, but He's finally realizing that it's impossible.**"**

(Patrice, age 11)

"The hardest thing for God to do is to see suffering happen. . . . He wishes that there was a way for us to learn our lessons without it.**"**

(Valerie, age 10)

Some of the Passing Thoughts that God Has About Us

"You can't tell those humans anything. . . . You would think they created the sun, the moon and the stars, instead of a bunch of time-saving gadgets and diet soft drinks."

(Tony, age 12)

"They're going to be shocked when they come up to Heaven and see that everything here is shared."

(Ron, age 12)

"I feel bad about that big flood and all the destruction. . . . I hope they have forgiven me for it."

(Gretchen, age 10)

"Why do they work so hard? Fifty hours a week, that's ridiculous. I never meant for that when I shut the door to paradise on them."

(Clark, age 11)

"It makes me sad that they hurt each other so much. . . . I wish they would step back and smell the flowers I created like we do in Heaven."

(Sandie, age 10)

"I wish I had a bigger refrigerator. . . . Then I could put drawings from all of the children of the world on it."

(Marie, age 6)

"People on Earth need to think more about religion than they do. . . . Maybe a set of Bible heroes cards would be very popular at the grocery store. . . . Hmm."

(Erich, age 11)

"Most of them mean well, but they're all the nervous types. . . . Don't they realize that I have a plan for each one of them?"

(Kyle, age 10)

"I wish they had classes in 'Being Kind' along with arithmetic and reading in the schools. . . . Then the kids would get to know Me even better."

(Eduardo, age 8)

"Maybe I gave them too much freedom?"

(Jeana, age 10)

"I'm glad they know that computers are just toys and people's feelings are what really counts."

(Sebastian, age 10)

"All those homeless people make Me sad. . . . I sure hope they keep the faith and keep believing that I'm making plenty of room for them in Heaven when it's their time. "

(Kirsten, age 10)

"I meant all of the people of the world to be fun and colorful, but those Americans are wilder than even I expected. "

(Nathaniel, age 9)

"I love all My children . . . but sometimes they give me the biggest headaches a God can have. "

(Yoki, age 9)

Does God Ever Visit Earth?

"Yes, He visits us in the summer. . . . In the winter He's in the Carribean."

(Koby, age 10)

"Of course God does. . . . We're a good change for Him if everything just seems too perfect in Heaven."

(Terence, age 9)

"God comes when He can find the time. He has a full schedule and He's in charge of five other galaxies, and they got their own problems."

(Russ, age 9)

"God visits Earth on Sundays. That's why we have church then."

(Zack, age 8)

"God likes to see us on Thanksgiving because God feels most appreciated then, and besides, turkey and stuffing is one of His favorite dishes."

(Byron, age 10)

"He comes to me when I sleep, and that's why I feel so good when I wake up in the morning. . . . God makes me feel safe."

(Corinne, age 6)

"God is around. He hangs out wherever there's people who want to talk with Him."

(Jack, age 8)

"I think God comes to Earth, but I probably miss Him because I'm in school so much of the time now."

(Kelly, age 6)

"God is everywhere, so I don't see any reason God wouldn't be in Boston. . . . And God might want to see where some of His angels started a revolution against the British king."

(Landon, age 10)

"We could probably get Him to come here more if we wrote Him more letters and sent Him fruitcakes."

(Kathleen, age 6)

"God in the world is pretty much an every-moment-of-the-day kind of thing."

(Carey, age 10)

Does God Have Any Second Thoughts About His Creations?

"Sure, but of course that would only be human of Him!"

(Sebastian, age 10)

"He wishes He made Heaven and Earth closer together to cut down on traveling costs."

(Phyllis, age 10)

"God never planned on television. . . . Now God is trying to get people's attention back."

(Joan, age 9)

"He might wish He hadn't created parts of New York and Washington."

(Carey, age 10)

"He likes the way some of the places near the ocean came out. . . . He thinks it's pretty there and He likes to bring seashells back to Heaven after His visits."

(Aretha, age 8)

"God isn't totally happy with Heaven either. . . . The men and the women are still arguing up there over who's smarter."

(Mary Beth, age 7)

"He wishes that earthquakes weren't so bad. They weren't supposed to be in the original plan, but God could never figure out how to make them less messy."

(Jackie, age 10)

"God is pleased that He made the animals before us, so then we shouldn't be surprised when they're the ones checking us in when we get to Heaven."

(Simone, age 11)

"He's happy with how many people give charity. . . . That's why He created good causes in the first place."

(Terence, age 9)

"God wants parents to teach more about Him. . . . He's working on having the parents less tired and having them home more hours."

(Walt, age 9)

"Giving us the power to make each other feel better was His best idea, and God is real proud of that one."

(Senji, age 9)

"On the whole, God is satisfied with us so long as we try to improve and remember that Heaven is a real place, not just a made-up land from a storybook."

(Tori, age 9)

Excerpts from God's Annual "State of Heaven" Address

"My assistants, Abraham and Joshua, have just given me an encouraging report: Idol worshipping is down by ten percent on all the planets.**"**

(Ron, age 12)

"My fellow Heaveners, Heaven is going pretty well. My new tests are screening out bad people. Now, I want to announce a new privilege: We are going to have Sprite in the cafeteria.**"**

(Carey, age 10)

"I appreciate all the letters I got from children this year. . . . With some of them, though, your hearts may be in the right place, but your spelling isn't.**"**

(Dariel, age 11)

"Hail Mary, I'm glad to see you sitting in the front row.**"**

(Tony, age 12)

"Friends, we're doing better than we did last century, but there's still more healing and miracles we need to do."

(Richie, age 9)

"I want to give a special tribute to the Angel Fred, who put out a fire in Nebraska last week. . . . Come fly up here and take a bow, Fred."

(Erich, age 11)

"My children, I am very pleased with the good work you are doing. But can't we do something about some of those know-it-all Republicans?"

(Jaymes, age 12)

"Just like past years, Our main job is to look after the sick. I need some volunteers to visit hospitals on Earth. . . . Well, I guess I'll have to draw straws, because it seems everybody in Heaven is raising their hands."

(Stacy, age 10)

"I plan to cut the taxes in Heaven. Everyone only has to give half as much fruit and vegetables from their gardens, as long as they keep giving the same amount of love."

(Senji, age 9)

"It's nice to see some of the recent dead people in the audience. . . . You see, didn't I tell you it would be worth the wait?"

(Landon, age 10)

"I appreciate all your prayers. They help me do My job as God. You might think that a God doesn't need any help, but let Me tell you, when the big decisions have to get made it gets pretty lonely on the mountain-top.**

(Kimberly, age 11)

What Are Prayers Like in Heaven?

"The people say: 'Our Father, who is right here with us. How is it going, Dad?'"

(Ron, age 12)

"They all gather around and pray that they are grateful to be in Heaven . . . not the other place."

(Carey, age 10)

"The new Heaven spirits pray to get picked as angels or shepherds and get picked for a secret mission for God."

(Ellie, age 8)

"If there is guys around in Heaven like my father, then they probably pray about their golf games."

(Shawn, age 8)

"More serious prayers . . . The people there don't pray about things like getting a toy tank for Christmas."

(Grant, age 10)

"Nobody in Heaven prays for themselves. . . . You pray for other people and hope like anything that somebody's doing the same for you."

(Keisha, age 9)

"Prayers in Heaven get answered faster—not because God is closer, but because the prayers are more sincere."

(Sharie, age 11)

"A lot of people pray for their relatives on the Earth. Like they say: 'Dear God, look after my cousin, Herbie. He's too lazy to get a job by himself.' "

(Jonathan, age 10)

"The people there pray for our souls because their souls are already at rest and snug with them."

(Carlos, age 9)

"God often leads them in prayers. He doesn't ask them for worship or nothing, just niceness toward all His creatures."

(Juliana, age 8)

"Some angels pray for new wings and others pray for more strength, but a lot of the prayers are for God, because He always has too much on His mind."

(Tim, age 10)

"All prayers in Heaven are basically for the same thing: peace on earth and goodwill toward men."

(Cory, age 11)

Is There a Favorite Religion in Heaven?

"ChristiJewishBuddalum . . . In Heaven, they take all the best ideas in the world and kinda glue them all together.**"**

(Erich, age 11)

" 'Deadism' is the main religion. . . . Their biggest belief is that their mission is to make the newly dead as comfortable and happy as possible.**"**

(Carey, age 10)

"I think maybe 'joy' is the main religious thing up there.**"**

(Rebecca, age 9)

"All religions are respected. . . . Angels aren't into prejudice; they are into halos and healing.**"**

(Kimberly, age 11)

"The only thing that we have that they don't have is doubt. . . . In Heaven they have seen the truth, and it's makin' them feel real good.**"**

(Stewart, age 9)

“God's favorite religion is any one that puts tons of importance on love and caring.”

(Marcus, age 11)

“The most favorite religion thing to do is take a walk with God. . . . It's a lot more laid back up there.”

(Terence, age 9)

“I think they still might take communion, but it's more like a big pizza than a cracker. . . . God wants people to enjoy themselves.”

(Daron, age 8)

“The churches are outdoors. . . . Since it never rains in Heaven, you can just pray in the sunshine all the time.”

(Brad, age 9)

“The angels have noticed that if they listen to God's teachings, their halos glow brighter and brighter. . . . So that's one of the big religious ceremonies up there, watchin' the angels glow in the dark.”

(Andrea, age 9)

“The religion differences are all over in Heaven. When you get there it's time to join hands and start singing 'Praise the Lord.' ”

(Jackie, age 10)

On Families in Heaven

"Angels help good parents to find Heaven, but the bad parents are on their own."

(Ellen, age 8)

"Families meet in Heaven and they live in a beautiful house that never needs repairs or the grass mowed."

(Josh, age 9)

"There are families of dogs in Heaven. . . . They bark like the devil when they get together again up there."

(David, age 11)

"It's all one big family in Heaven, and the people of Heaven of all ages just call God 'Papa' when they see Him."

(Bobbi, age 9)

"Heaven wants families to stay together at all times. . . . That's why God is glad those phone companies keep making it easier to call long distance."

(Jenny, age 9)

"Heaven is something like the circus because it's a happy, family kind of place . . . except maybe the food is better in Heaven and it smells nicer up there."

(Arnie, age 8)

"Heaven is for families because to God we are all part of the same family . . . and He loves us all."

(Marian, age 9)

Is Heaven Just for Dead People?

"If it isn't just a place for the dead, then I bet there would be a big traffic jam to get in every weekend."

(Nathaniel, age 9)

"I heard there was a city in Vermont named Heaven, but I don't think you can fly around up there."

(Toren, age 7)

"Heaven is a place for all believers . . . but to tell you the truth, you might feel a little out of place if you aren't dead yet."

(Tim, age 10)

"I guess most of Heaven is something you find out about later on, but if you go to church, they might give you a few hints right now."

(Mert, age 9)

"We can find out about Heaven here . . . not through an encyclopedia, but through being with people in a real caring way."

(Gerold, age 12)

"Heaven is anywhere God comes to us and says hello."

(Mindy, age 6)

"Since God created us and He's a big part of Heaven, it must be around us all of the time."

(Carey, age 10)

Will Heaven Be Boring?

"No, where else are you going to be such a free spirit?"

(Lisa, age 12)

"I think it could be interesting even if there are no Power Rangers there."

(Eileen, age 7)

"Before I can answer that I need to know how long the sermons are in Heaven."

(Duncan, age 9)

"It's fun there! You can play hopscotch with the spirits, and both of you can jump over clouds."

(Donna, age 7)

"I think it's really Satan who is boring. . . . Imagine wearing red all the time!"

(Caren, age 9)

"There's plenty of talking lions and zebras who just came back to life there, so I think it would be a lot of fun to be in Heaven."

(Philip, age 6)

"No, not boring at all. You get to talk with God, and He might even tell you some of His miracle secrets."

(Janine, age 8)

"If you are curious, you'll never be bored in Heaven. Just ask God things like: 'How did you pick color schemes for the world? Also, God, why did you create people of different colors?'"

(Mollie, age 11)

"Eternity could be fun if there is a swimming pool and tennis courts there . . . and oh yeah, if there's nice people there too."

(Gerry, age 11)

Should We Be Eager to Get to Heaven or Concentrate on Life Here on Earth?

"We should relax and try to figure out what we should eat for lunch and not worry about stuff like that."

(William, age 7)

"I'm eager . . . I want to see if God will take me on His knee and give me a ride."

(Camille, age 7)

"I'm not in a hurry. I'm only six and I want to see if I can ever drive a car first."

(Heidi, age 6)

"Probably most people would just as soon not be dead yet. . . . There's plenty of time for that later on."

(Dianna, age 8)

"Heaven would be really cool if you didn't have to have a heart attack first to get there."

(Annie, age 8)

"I can't wait to see if I am going to turn out to be a big angel or just a regular spirit eating fruit and lying in one of those hammocks."

(Terence, age 9)

"I guess Heaven is supposed to be better than Earth, but who can top sleeping late on Saturdays and still having a mom who makes breakfast for you?"

(Dave, age 8)

"God wants us to ask for Heaven in our prayers. . . . That's why He wrote the word 'Heaven' in the hymns and stories. He wants us not to forget about it."

(Sharie, age 11)

"Like my father says: 'We should just take this life one day at a time.' "

(Marilee, age 8)

"I sure hope to join God, but not just yet. . . . I hope to play at the top level of Little League next year."

(Brendan, age 9)

"It doesn't matter whether you are here or in Heaven, you should just keep trying to be the best person you can be . . . and that's the biggest truth."

(Leslie, age 9)

How Might We Make Our World More Like Heaven?

"Invite God for a sleepover."

(Bethany, age 7)

"If there were no fences between people."

(Bryant, age 8)

"Start your own garden like the big, beautiful one that is in Heaven."

(Marian, age 9)

"Learn to play with all different kinds of people. . . . Even if you're in the fourth grade, try to play with third-graders."

(Bill, age 9)

"Let Mary and Joseph be role models for you . . . and hope your child turns out like their child did."

(Deb, age 9)

"Save the forests by placing a guardian angel over each one."

(Blaine, age 9)

"No killing, no car pollution and no crab grass. . . . I know the third one isn't important, but it drives my father nuts and I like to keep the guy happy."

(Ron, age 10)

"When you pray, pray for others and ask others to pray for you."

(Jenny, age 9)

"Celebrate all the positive things in life. . . . A day with your best friend is one of them."

(Katie, age 8)

"Every time you see a dark cloud in your life, remember that clouds are part of Heaven too."

(Lisa, age 12)

The One Thing Above All Others that Is Definitely "Heavenly"

"All grandmothers."

(Bobbi, age 9)

"Carrots . . . It's a miracle that a little thing like that can make your eyes feel better."

(Douglas, age 7)

"I was going to say Heavenly Hash ice cream, but I think love might be more important."

(Roger, age 10)

"When a person stands up in the world and really tries to stop prejudice."

(John, age 7)

"Just being around a lot of nice people who really like you. . . . They don't have to be angels, just friends."

(Sidney, age 7)

"A church is like Heaven . . . but only if the people's prayers are sincere."

(Joseph, age 10)

"A beautiful sunset . . . especially when it happens at the beginning of school vacation week and you know you have a lot of fun ahead of you."

(Danielle, age 9)

"Kisses are supposed to be like Heaven. . . . I hear they are supposed to make you feel on top of the world."

(Charlotta, age 10)

"The first snowfall makes me think of Heaven. . . . The flakes are like diamonds falling from the sky."

(Mollie, age 11)

"A home is like Heaven . . . if it's filled with caring and love."

(Claire, age 10)

On the Purpose of
Heaven and Angels

"Heaven is there because people need a change of scenery after they have been walking around on the Earth for ninety years!"

(Rikki, age 11)

"Heaven is for relaxing and for eating all the cheeseburgers you want."

(Martin, age 8)

"It's to give us hope. . . . Just because you have to die doesn't mean you have to be dead forever, just for a little while."

(Bobbi, age 9)

"Everybody needs to know where to pray to. . . . Just praying to people would be silly, because you can see they aren't perfect and they got problems of their own."

(Dayle, age 7)

"Heaven and angels help you against evil. . . . Like if somebody tries to trip you, an angel might be there to make sure the kid gets a sore leg just in the 'nick of time.' **"**

(Scott, age 9)

"Heaven is there because God wants us to have a nice place to retire . . . plus that way, older grandparents can see the whole world and they don't have to get tired from buses and trains.**"**

(Vance, age 8)

"They are there to take away all hurts and wounds and make everything better for people.**"**

(Carey, age 10)

"They're symbols of peace. . . . Peace is something we can use more of, because the world down here is pretty confusing sometimes.**"**

(Greg, age 12)

"God and Heaven are there for us so that we have somebody at our side at all times—we are never really alone.**"**

(Simone, age 11)

On Belief

"If you don't believe in Heaven, then you'll have no place to play after you leave the Earth."

(Maria, age 9)

"Believing in Heaven is like believing there could be an end to meanness. . . . Count me in on that."

(Ryan, age 10)

"It's good to believe in Heaven. . . . Who knows? You might end up there someday."

(Kala, age 7)

"When we believe in Heaven real strong we shine like lights, and God is able to see us and look after us better."

(Rich, age 8)

"It's a good idea to believe in Heaven because then, later on, it won't come as a big surprise to you and give you a heart attack."

(Shonte, age 10)

"Most of the people I know believe in Heaven. . . . You might say that we're just kids, but then maybe God just talks to us more often."

(Michael, age 10)

Concluding Reflections on Heaven

"Heaven is a good place to pray to. . . . They got more answers up there."

(Ty, age 8)

"I think I would like Heaven. . . . I hear it's even prettier than New England."

(Bobbi, age 9)

"You don't need a ticket to get into Heaven. . . . All that you need is goodness."

(Debi, age 10)

"It ought to be crowded up there by now. Unless a lot of people are flunking out and having to repeat life."

(Roger, age 10)

"I wish my family had a summer house there. Then I could see what Heaven was like and still get back to see my friends in September."

(Peter, age 8)

"Heaven is all that really matters. Everything else is kinda for now, but Heaven is for today and tomorrow and for every day after that too."

(Lorraine, age 11)

"Heaven is where we are all headed . . . but some people must like to take their time gettin' there."

(Mark, age 10)

"You know, it might not be in the sky. . . . I think it's very possible that Heaven might be right inside your heart."

(Jenny, age 9)

So Let It Be Said: "God Is in Heaven and . . ."

"He's inside our house too.**"**

(Amy, age 6)

"He's playing 'Jeopardy' there. . . . The Bible is His favorite category.**"**

(Shonte, age 10)

"So is anybody else who ever helped a person in need.**"**

(David, age 11)

"His angels are spread out all over the world making sure little children and big people over twenty-five are safe at night.**"**

(Andrea, age 7)

"What's-his-name is down in the dungeon where he belongs.**"**

(Marcy, age 8)

"God is resting. . . . He's older than He used to be, and just because you're forever doesn't mean you don't need a nap sometimes."

(Ryan, age 10)

"Our day will come too."

(Dan, age 10)

"But His love has long-distance power that makes it all the way down to us . . . and I'm sure glad it does."

(Mark, age 10)

About the Authors

David Heller, Ph.D. has authored a number of successful books, including *Talking to Your Child About God, The Soul of a Man, Dear God: Children's Letters to God, Just Build the Ark and the Animals Will Come, Love Is Like a Crayon Because It Comes In All Colors* and *My Mother Is the Best Gift I Ever Got.* His work concerning religion and family communication has been featured all across the country, including segments on "20/20" and CNBC, and articles in *People, Parents, Good Housekeeping, Catholic Digest, Redbook, USA Today, Psychology Today, Parenting* and in nationally syndicated pieces for Universal Press Syndicate. He graduated from Harvard and the University of Michigan, and has taught at both as well. He is currently a Senior Clinical Fellow at The Boston Institute for Psychotherapy.

Elizabeth Heller, M.S. is the author of the inspirational book, *Little Lessons of Love,* and has co-authored *The Best Christmas Presents are Wrapped in Heaven, Grandparents Are Made for Hugging* and *A Kids' Book of Prayers About All Sorts of Things.* She has developed a children's news program for cable TV, and produced and hosted a radio show for children on WBZ in Boston. Elizabeth has also served as Director of Research for World Monitor News on the Discovery Channel and Director of Public Relations for Catholic Charities. She holds a Bachelors degree in English from Santa Clara and a Masters degree in Journalism from Boston University.